THE KINDNESS ALCHEMIST

By

LEO ALAZA

INDIA • SINGAPORE • MALAYSIA

ISBN 979-8-89588-903-9

For whom this book is seeking.

Contents

Alchemy focuses on the ability of one element to morph into another. A peace of into gold or something else of value. It's the science of mixing things to make new things. Some say it's impossible. Some call it magic. The alchemist, always ignoring the sceptics and the narrow-minded, attempts the impossible, experimenting with different elements in the pursuit of transformation. The 1600s and 1700s were the golden age of alchemy. You may have come from this proud lineage and carry the true mark of an alchemist, someone with the ability to transform, to create, to lead, and to heal.

Preface

Alchemy is a spiritual belief in ancient times that was partly experimentation and partly magic. An alchemist would turn base materials into precious ones, like gold or silver. In our modern world, alchemy sounds a bit ridiculous but its concept and belief that things can be changed into something of higher value remain timeless.

The world is constantly changing. It has always been. However, the question is: have the changes been serving the highest good of all life forms? Different people have different answers depending on who you ask.

It got me thinking about how we can change the world to be a better place than it has been, where all its power systems and structures support our true existential purpose; how we can transform the way humans think and behave on the planet where life only thrives in co-existence, and anything that goes against this principle will only be destructive, how we can turn apathy to empathy, and from empathy to compassion.

This is not a new thought though. From the great ancient mystics, the philosophers down to the thinkers and people with broader spiritual perspectives of our time – all have taught us about the importance of change and transformation based on the virtues of love, empathy, compassion and kindness.

It will take great works of alchemy to create a new world where all these virtues shine. But never has this been more possible than in the present time. The advancement of science and technology has helped create an opportunity for all alchemists of the world to merge. Their combined knowledge in the art of change-making will give birth to a super alchemy that could potentially transform the world.

These alchemists are the many known and unknown individuals in the world who, having experienced the process of self-transformation themselves, have been trying to make a difference in the world.

"This is why alchemy exist," the boy said. "So that everyone will search for his treasure, find it, and then want to be better than he was in his former life...That's what alchemists do. They show that, when we strive to become better than we are, everything around us becomes better too."

– Paolo Coelho, The Alchemist

CHAPTER 01

A Silent Cry for a Kinder World

"Well everybody hurts sometimes."

– R.E.M, American rock band

Recently, I saw a short video of Steve Burns, the original host of the popular American interactive educational children's television series, 'Blue's Clues'. Something about the video moved me. It's hard to describe the feeling. Perhaps helplessness is the closest that I can think of.

'Blue's Clues' premiered on Nickelodeon's Nick Jr. block on September 8, 1996. Upon debuting, it became the highest-rated show for preschoolers on American commercial television and was critical to Nickelodeon's growth. It has been syndicated in 120 countries and translated into 15 languages. By 2002, Blue's Clues had received several awards for excellence in children's programming, educational software and licensing, and had been nominated for nine Emmy Awards.

In that same year, it was reported to be one of the highest-rated shows for preschoolers, preschool children and their parents' favorite cable preschool programme.

It was viewed by approximately 13.7 million viewers each week and aired in about 60 countries.

'Blue's Clues' features Burns welcoming his preschool audience to a house where his animated puppy, Blue, helps find three clues to something they are trying to figure out. Viewers are invited to participate, with Blue and her friends stopping to listen to what the audience has to say.

The creators and producers' mission of 'Blue's Clues' was to "empower, challenge, and build the self-esteem of preschoolers ... while making them laugh."

'Blue's Clues' co-creator and producer Angela Santomero said: "I wanted so much to give kids a television show that celebrates how smart they are, because I truly believe they are brilliant. I also wanted to create a show that would help preschoolers feel good about themselves".

In the video, Burns, who is now 51 years old, appeared with a sombre and compassionate look on his face, a complete opposite of his cheerful and fun character that children all over the world had grown to love in the six years he was on the show.

"Hello, what's going on? How are you? What's new?" Next came on screen some of the 139,681 comments as Burns read them attentively.

– *I'm tired, Steve. I need a hug.*
– *Hi Steve. I'm still alive. I stayed.*

- *Steve...I'm losing it here. I'm tired of being an adult.*
- *Ohh Steve life is falling apart. I wish we could go back to look for clues.*
- *Oh Steve. My husband was diagnosed with prostate cancer Tuesday and I'm scared.*
- *Life is lifeing Steve. You didn't prepare me for this.*

They were once innocent kids who are now adults. They speak for millions of others who are suffering in silence in a world that has become increasingly unkind. Often, we don't have the words to express our pain. The most we can do is to numb it. It's sad because this is not the way we want to live this short life on Earth. How much we want life to treat us kindly; that the political and economic systems, the technological advancements serve our highest good. We want to live a happy and peaceful life. It's not too much to ask for. But happiness and peace are just a state of being when we pretend the suffering and pain are not there.

Sometimes, we feel we want to do something to change all of this. But when we don't know where to turn to or where to start, we feel helpless and defeated. So, we return to what we do best, numbing and pretending as if everything is alright and wait for the next hit of happiness and peace.

But seriously, we can break this chain. We are more powerful than we think because we are capable of doing alchemy. We can use it to transform ordinary things into 'gold'. We can make this world kinder.

"I think probably kindness is my number one attribute in a human being. I'll put it before any of the things like courage, bravery, generosity, or anything else... Kindness—that simple word. To be kind—it covers everything, to my mind. If you're kind, that's it."

– Roald Dahl, author

1.1 Remembering Our Power

*"There are three ways to ultimate success:
The first way is to be kind. The second way is
to be kind. The third way is to be kind."*

– Fred Rogers, television host, author and producer

So, we want to know the secret of making this world kinder. But first, we must understand why kindness is very powerful and why all this while we didn't see it. We all want to be treated kindly because kindness was the first human act we experienced when we were born. We may not remember that moment, but we have seen many times how a newborn child feels safe in the arms of its mother and father. That feeling is the feeling of kindness. Wrapped in this energy, it trusts that everything will be alright. There is no fear, even for a child who is born in the war zone. So, this is how the world welcomes each one of us, with kindness. This is the forgotten secret.

As we get older, we gradually learn the ways of the world. In this world, the systems and structures have been created in such a way that only the strongest and fittest will survive. In a fierce environment where we must constantly compete to earn our place, kindness is perceived as a sign of weakness. So, we fight like slave gladiators to the death for dear life, completely oblivious to the truth that none of us is the opponent. This duel of ours has always been for the purpose of others watching from the stands of the colosseum; the wealthy and powerful elites. We know we don't have to be at their mercy, but we are busy fighting for our lives to think much about it.

Four years ago, all of us, irrespective of our social status, were forced to fight a common enemy that was invisible to the naked eye. Men, women, children, the elderly, rich and poor – all of us were inside the fighting ring, fearing death on a massive scale. But in truth, the pain from the loss of our freedom was greater than the fear of death. Self-imprisoned by our own doing, we turned to kindness for hope, comfort and safety. It was as if the human collective crawled back to the arms of mother and father, where kindness was first felt. It was then the entire world witnessed the power of kindness in its glory.

There has been a lot of talk that the world after Covid-19 is unlikely to return to the world that was. Many trends already underway in the global power systems and structures have been accelerated by the impact of the pandemic. The old world has been disrupted to make way for what some call a new global order.

However, for people who understand the real purpose and meaning of change, the way forward for the world is to make kindness not only a norm but a global order. This is not some bedtime they-live-happily-ever-after fairytale story. This is a proven and tested human collective power we can use to save ourselves from further ruin.

"In any given moment we have two options: to step forward into growth or step back into safety."

– Abraham Maslow, psychologist

CHAPTER 02

Dare to Dream a Kinder World

"The secret of change is to focus all your energy not on fighting the old, but on building the new"

– Socrates

If you're reading this, chances are you've been called to change the world. You are an alchemist.

You're one of the millions of individuals who have a big kind heart to make a difference in the lives of others. You believe all of us are born into the world to live a good life, not one that is full of hardships, suffering, and uncertainties. In your mind, goodness is a divine gift, whereas hardships are man-made.

As things stand, life on the planet has become increasingly challenging for billions of people. Despite the advancement of technology, people are struggling to meet their basic needs. The issues of rising food prices and food safety, unaffordable homes and lack of job opportunities are just some of the many challenges that people are struggling with. People turn to leaders for hope that things will get better. They have not. When the powers in the political, economic and social systems are not making life any kinder for us, we return to kindness to make us powerful. It is a virtue all of us can agree on. It's our universal shared identity. When we use the power to create systems that support our existence, the planet will stand a chance of becoming a kinder place for all.

Changing the world is in fact a work in progress by nations and many social movements in the world. Their commitment is very relevant today as global citizens are increasingly concerned with so many issues. Many countries are grappling with inflation, supply chain disruptions, rising costs of living, social issues like injustices and land grabbing. Technological advances that, although many claim to be beneficial, have caused painful job loss for many people who must feed their families. Geopolitical tensions that could potentially start a big war. Unexplained natural disasters. Political polarization. Religious tensions. The list of problems is long.

Problems like these are nothing new to the world. They have always been there for centuries. However, people are increasingly sensing that there is a dark and wicked force behind all the world's problems. That the problems are meant to serve a purpose: control.

The quest for control has in fact always been there in our human history. Control over territories, resources, cultures and people. Today, with technology increasingly taking a life and power of its own, the lust for control can be frightening. The history of domination and control is full of suffering and pain. And death. Conquerors like Alexander The Great, Genghis Khan, Napoleon Bonaparte and Hitler would not have achieved their aim if they had acted with kindness and compassion. Kindness, compassion and empathy do not exist in the vocabulary of a conqueror. All conquests tell the same story of chaos, suffering, pain and confusion to fulfil someone's lust for power and glory. I often wonder what the world would have become today if all Indigenous Peoples' cultures, traditions and sacred territories had not been destroyed by colonial powers. I believe it would have been a much better world otherwise some world leaders would not have issued a public apology for centuries of mistreatment, and acknowledged that the ancient wisdom of the Indigenous Peoples could offer solutions to some of the complex modern problems.

The human appetite for domination and conquest continues as manifested by the problems the world is facing today. If we look closely, a lot of things that are going on come down to a contest for power, resources and territory, either physical or digital. And as history has shown us, things can get ugly. Things can get unkind. While problems will always be there, we can resist anything that is harmful to our existence. We can alchemise and change things.

I wanted to inspire all those who believe they've been chosen for this mission, all the alchemists in the world. So, here's what I've come up with: a short book for changemakers who want to do something within their power to contribute to change. It's a book that specifically touches on kindness as a unifying and guiding force that governs the way we live with one another on this planet.

In chapter 13, I proposed some practical steps on how the concept of kindness as a power for global transformation could be realised in actions. One of the ideas is to pilot what I call a Kindness Landscape Approach that brings like-minded stakeholders within the boundary of a landscape to push kindness as an agenda for development.

You're not alone for there are millions of others just like you. I've been thinking if there's a way all the like-minded souls could unite, the world could be a strong force to take on any powerful troublemakers with an agenda.

No one says this will be easy. It has never been. But the human collective has reached a critical point where it's more painful to simply let life happen to us than to create the life we want. International self-development coach Anthony Robbins says: "Change happens when the pain of staying the same is greater than the pain of change."

“When you hit rock bottom, the only way to go is up”

– Unknown

CHAPTER 03

The Bottom Must Rise

"If you think you are too small to make a difference, try sleeping with a mosquito."

– Dalai Lama

In a brief published in 2022, Oxfam International revealed that the pandemic had created a new billionaire every 30 hours. For every billionaire created, nearly a million people could be pushed into extreme poverty in that year, nearly at the same rate.

The brief, titled 'Profiting From Pain', was published to coincide with the World Economic Forum, which the organisation described as the exclusive get-together of the global elites, that was taking place in Davos, Switzerland.

"Billionaires are arriving in Davos to celebrate an incredible surge in their fortunes. The pandemic and now steep increase in food and energy prices have, simply put, been a bonanza for them. Meanwhile, decades of progress on extreme poverty are now in reverse and millions of people are facing impossible rises in the cost of simply staying alive," said Gabriela Bucher, the Executive Director of Oxfam International, which is an international confederation of 21 NGOs working with partners in over 90 countries to end injustices that cause poverty.

The brief showed that 573 people became new billionaires during the pandemic. In 2022, it was expected that 263 million more people would fall into extreme poverty, at a rate of a million people every 33 hours.

The brief revealed that billionaires' wealth had risen more in the first 24 months of COVID-19 than in 23 years combined, and that the total wealth of the world's billionaires was then equivalent to 13.9 percent of global GDP. This was a threefold increase (up from 4.4 percent) in 2000.

"Billionaires' fortunes have not increased because they are now smarter or working harder. Workers are working harder, for less pay and in worse conditions. The super-rich have rigged the system with impunity for decades and they are now reaping the benefits. They have seized a shocking amount of the world's wealth as a result of privatization and monopolies, gutting regulation and workers' rights while stashing their cash in tax havens — all with the complicity of governments."

"Meanwhile, millions of others are skipping meals, turning off the heating, falling behind on bills and wondering what they can possibly do next to survive. Across East Africa, one person is likely dying every minute from hunger. This grotesque inequality is breaking the bonds that hold us together as humanity. It is divisive, corrosive and dangerous. This is inequality that literally kills," Bucher added.

Oxfam International also reported that the pandemic had created 40 new pharma billionaires. As expected, some have been skeptical about the findings.

If all these findings indicate that things have not been going right with the world, then people need to question if the United Nations' 'Leave No One Behind (LNOB) transformative promise to the world means anything. Because it appears that with the widening gulf between extreme wealth and extreme poverty, most of the people on this planet are being left behind. And looking at the wealth figures, I can't see how they are able to catch up.

After reading the brief, I took out the calculator and tried to figure out how many millions of people would have been pushed down to the bottom in 2024. I stopped halfway. It was too depressing.

The question is: Can we do something to help reduce the gap? Or find alternative models where someone's richness does not make another person poorer? Our quick response might be that it is not an easy question to answer. This is if we think of solutions individually and within the limitations of our knowledge and experience. But what if millions and billions of people ask the same question? What if millions and billions of people look for an answer together? This will certainly take the question into the mainstream and to a place of more relevance and power. However, the problem is that when people don't ask questions, they won't seek answers or solutions. When people don't ask why the rich are getting richer and the poor are getting poorer, nothing happens. It'll be just business as usual in the world. Except for individuals who have an interest in the issue, not many ordinary people in the world have ever read Oxfam International's shocking findings.

The only way down is up. We, the little people at the bottom, are in fact more powerful than we think. We have been made powerless by our own limited beliefs. Some of us are familiar with the Roger Bannister Effect. It is a phenomenon that describes someone who could do something that was deemed impossible to do, which encouraged many people to follow through after breaking the psychological barrier. The effect was named after Roger Bannister, the British track and field icon who, on May 6, 1954, became the first athlete to finish the mile run in under four minutes. Before he set the record, many believed it was impossible. Today, thousands of people have achieved it. The mind does create reality.

Many people throughout history have conquered the impossible and paved the way for those who came after them to break the boundaries that were once unthinkable.

We may find it a challenge to campaign for a kinder world by ourselves, but collectively we can do wonders. I think we can learn a lot from our fellow planet dwellers, the ants. One single ant might seem very tiny and weak. But a whole colony can achieve greatness.

"Change will not come if we wait for some other person or some other time. We are the ones we've been waiting for. We are the change that we seek."

– Barack Obama, Former US President.

3.1 The Power of the Common People

"Never doubt that a small group of thoughtful, committed, citizens can change the world. Indeed, it is the only thing that ever has."

– Margaret Mead, Cultural anthropologist, author and speaker.

The revolt of the gladiator Spartacus in 73-71 BCE stands out as the most successful slave revolt in the history of Rome. Known as the Third Servile War, the rebellion was the last of three major slave revolts. Contrary to how he was portrayed as a freedom fighter in books and films, Spartacus was just a common man who could no longer tolerate the Roman institution of slavery. Slavery was widespread in ancient Rome. Slaves were used for many different tasks in all the different sectors like agriculture, manufacturing, construction and households. According to the historian Plutarch, the original plan of the gladiators was to escape. But the plan was discovered so they had no choice but to fight for freedom or submit to execution.

The world has seen several revolutions that shaped history. By the late 18th century, the people of France were living in an extremely dirty and unpleasant environment due to extreme poverty, all except the nobility who lived lavish and expensive lifestyles. Frustrated with a monarchy that collected heavy taxes but offered nothing in return, the citizenry turned their widespread discontent on King Louis XVI. During this period, French citizens radically altered their political landscape, uprooting centuries-old institutions such as the monarchy and the feudal system. The upheaval was caused by disgust with the French aristocracy and the economic policies of King Louis XVI. He was publicly executed by beheading, as was his wife Marie Antoinette. The French Revolution helped to shape modern democracies by showing the power inherent in the will of the people.

In 1917, the Russian Revolution of 1917 marked the end of the Romanov dynasty and centuries of Russian Imperial rule. Economic hardship, food shortages and government corruption all contributed to disillusionment with Czar Nicholas II. During the Russian Revolution, the Bolsheviks, led by leftist revolutionary Vladimir Lenin, seized power and destroyed the tradition of czarist rule. The Bolsheviks would later become the Communist Party of the Soviet Union.

Other revolutions include the English Revolution (1649), American Revolution (1776), French and Chinese Revolutions (1949), all of which share a similar characteristic – they challenge the status quo.

However, in more recent times, we have witnessed mass protests, but they were not revolutionary. 2019 saw several protests in the world. In Chile, an estimated one million people joined a peaceful protest march in the capital, calling on the government to tackle inequality.

Hong Kong witnessed the largest series of demonstrations in its history against the Hong Kong government's introduction of a bill to amend the Fugitive Offenders Ordinance in regard to extradition. They then spread to reflect wider demands for democratic reform, and an inquiry into alleged police brutality. In Iraq, protests erupted in Baghdad and in several Shiite provinces in the south over unemployment, government corruption and the lack of basic services – such as electricity and clean water. Many Iraqis blamed the political parties in power for their economic hardship and the scale of the protests, believed to be the biggest since the fall of former Iraqi President Saddam Hussein in 2003, took the government by surprise.

I do not condone violent protests, but I think we can always learn from these painful events. One of them is that when people are pushed into hardships, they will unite and rise. Civil rights leader, Dr Martin Luther King Jr once said during his "Keep on Moving" speech in May 1963, "There is power in unity, and there is power in numbers." His famous quote remains true today for individuals, families and communities who feel that they must come together as a powerful force for change. When people work together, they are much more powerful than they would be apart, and this is what creates change.

But mass protests do not have to be violent. As a teenager back in 1986, I witnessed what was dubbed the "People Power" movement in the Philippines when millions of Filipinos marched in the streets of Manila in peaceful protest and prayer to overthrow the Marcos regime. I watched the historic event on television at a friend's house. Although I was very young to understand politics, I remember thinking that the people must have suffered a lot of pain until they saw no other way but to come together in large numbers to force their government to its knees. Some of the visuals of the event remain fresh in my mind. I saw the protestors praying and giving flowers to soldiers. It wasn't our normal understanding of what power is. It was the power of peace and kindness.

In her groundbreaking research, Erica Chenoweth, a political scientist at Harvard, found that nonviolent campaigns are twice as likely to achieve their goals as violent campaigns. She has shown that it takes around 3.5% of the population to actively participate in the protests to ensure serious political change.

"I am no longer accepting the things I cannot change. I am changing the things I cannot accept."

– Angela Davis, political activist

3.2 Kindness is a Weapon

"May your weapon be kindness. Your shield compassion. May the flowers grow again to sprout love from all this sadness."

– Courtney Peppernell, Australian author

Expressing rage and anger is not a wise way to push the global kindness agenda. It would be like putting a gun to someone's head and telling him to be kind. He will do it only because his life is under threat. For kindness to become the new currency in the world, there has to be a fundamental change in the way of thinking about or visualizing something. Polish astronomer, Nicolaus Copernicus' ideas revolutionized the way people viewed man's place in the universe, as he proposed the heliocentric model with the Sun at the centre of the solar system. This challenged the belief in geocentrism and shifted the focus away from Earth, showing that humans were not the centre of the universe.

History shows that the 300-year period of the Renaissance, the Scientific Revolution and the Protestant Reformation between the 15th to the 18th centuries had been a significant era of thought revolution with many philosophical and political changes happening quite rapidly. People expanded their worldviews as they expanded their knowledge of new concepts and accepted new ideas. It was the time when most countries in Europe had absolute monarchies. Over time, people began to question the power of absolute governments and as their discontentment grew, the questions turned to protests. And protests became full blown revolutions which changed the political systems and public belief.

I believe the global acts of kindness we witnessed during the pandemic have fundamentally changed our way of thinking about taking care of one another on a massive scale. More than just a reaction to pain, uncertainty and loss of freedom, it was a resistance to existential threats. Kindness was our weapon.

In today's more complex and interconnected world, I'm sure citizens are questioning a lot more about what has been going on in the world. People are digging deeper for answers. But without a common agenda, their efforts will only result in expressions of rage and anger. They will end up shooting blanks. All their actions will become powerful when they can come together under a big alliance of global kindness movements.

"Kindness is not an act. It's a lifestyle."

– Anthony Douglas Williams,
writer and animal rights activist

3.3 Kindness Beyond Random Acts

"It's easy to make a buck. It's a lot harder to make a difference."

– Tom Brokaw, journalist and author

Some friends of mine volunteer in a soup kitchen every Saturday. They cook chicken rice, pack it and deliver each one to the poor in the neighbourhood. Their average number is 200 people which is a lot of work. I salute them for their commitment and generosity. But I'm thinking if they could do more than that. Maybe instead of just feeding the poor, they could develop innovative ways to address the issue of poverty. We all know the phrase, "Give a man a fish and you feed him for a day. Teach a man how to fish, and feed him for a lifetime."

In the popular sitcom, 'The Big Bang Theory', the billionaire businessman, Elon Musk, makes a cameo appearance as a volunteer in a soup kitchen on Thanksgiving Day. In his conversation with the character Howard, played by Simon Helberg, he says, "It feels great to come down here and help the less fortunate." It is only a film, and Musk was obviously following lines prepared for him by the directors. But just for the sake of driving my point, he, being one of the richest men in the world, could have made a huge difference in the global fight against poverty and hunger than just washing dishes and serving food in a soup kitchen.

I know some of my soup kitchen volunteer friends are wealthy and successful people. They are in the position to do a lot more if they want to. Aside from volunteering to feed people a packet of chicken rice once a week, they might want to consider implementing community socio-economic upliftment programmes to empower people to become more financially independent. But here lies the issue with kindness; that they seem to be more about the giver than the recipients. Being kind makes them feel good, feel healthier, meaningful existence. But that doesn't have the same impact on people who receive an act of kindness. In the case of the recipients of the chicken rice donations, they get a temporary relief, but it doesn't solve their pain of poverty. If the volunteers could use their business experience and knowledge to help them, it would not only demonstrate the real power of kindness, but it will also make big and long-lasting and life-changing impacts. However, the rich and powerful don't necessarily have to make a difference to people's lives for the good of the society and the world. Some of them probably would. For the ones who do, they have the mind of an alchemist, a changemaker. They believe in the human collective power to change the world.

On June 30, 2024, a devastating flash flood destroyed everything that my family owned. Along with all our personal belongings, it wiped out many items of sentimental value. It felt almost like our past was erased and now we must start afresh. Although the old wooden house, built by my wife's late father with his own bare hands 64 years ago, withstood the full force of the 14 feet of water, it is now no longer conducive and safe for living. It would cost us a lot of money to do repairs, but even if we decided to do it, there is no telling when the next flood is going to hit and how big it will be. My wife, Rita, and I are temporarily renting a room. Our two sons who are in their early 20s are sharing a tiny apartment. This is the way our life is for now and we just have to make the best of it.

Many kind-hearted individuals reached out to hundreds of the flood victims, donating food, water, clothes and cash. Many people also offered to help clean the victims' houses. My family and I were left with only the clothes we wore the day the flood came, our phones and some personal documents in our wallets. Some of our close relatives, friends and even strangers were quick to offer us some cash donations we are forever grateful for. The display of public kindness at the time when many people were suffering heavy losses was reminiscent of the time of the pandemic. I remember one moment when I received a notification on my phone that some money had been credited to my account. It was a donation from a friend of a friend who wanted to remain anonymous. At that moment, I said to Rita that the world was never short of kind-hearted people.

However, there is another side of kindness that was not visible in relation to the flood. It's kindness activism, the one that questions the root cause of the disaster that had caused hundreds of families so much suffering and pain. It's the side of kindness that kicks butts. Some people in public speculated that the flood, which took a woman's life, was caused by hill cutting activities, massive land clearing, and land reclaiming. During a previous big flood that hit a couple of years ago, a local activist flew his drone to capture evidence of such activities. Despite all the public speculations and evidence-backed expose by the activist, nothing has improved. Things only got a lot worse. The June flood was the biggest we had ever experienced.

Another issue that hardly anyone with access to the government was talking about was the huge water bill incurred by flood victims. Their water consumption was unusually high due to all the heavy cleaning they had to do. It would be a great act of kindness on the part of the government to at least offer the victims some discounts to ease their burden. Of course, a government is not a charity organisation. But it could always bend bureaucracy to make way for kindness.

Several years ago, while discussing some issues that people had been making noise about, a politician friend said to me: "When we can't solve a difficult problem, it's best that we just keep quiet. People will forget. They always do."

His Holiness the 17th Gyalwang Karmapa, Ogyen Trinley Dorje says, "The most dangerous thing in the world is apathy. We think of weapons, violence, warfare, disease as terrible dangers, and indeed they are, but we can take measures to avoid them. But once our apathy takes hold of us, we can no longer avoid it."

(As I'm writing, my thoughts and prayers go to the families and victims who are suffering from the devastating impact of Hurricane Helene that hit North Carolina and Hurricane Milton in Florida, in the United States.)

I hope this short book will inspire people around the world, especially the emerging generation of thought leaders who think alike, to push the kindness agenda as the basis of human existence. As many believe that one single act of kindness can create ripples to change the world. Imagine its power when it is multiplied into billions of acts. And imagine its force when kindness becomes the one single human act to create a new world order. This would be a great work of alchemy.

I have asked random people in the streets if they believed there should be more kindness in society. Not a single one of them disagreed. I believe this is true all over the world because kindness is a universal concept acceptable by everyone. It is often the battle cry of the oppressed. Amid all the chaos, the darkness and wickedness of the world, kindness gives light and power. The famous writer, Mark Twain, says, "Kindness is the language which the deaf can hear and the blind can see."

Not long ago, Rita, and I were taking a walk down the street, and we saw a couple feeding a pregnant stray cat.

We approached them to offer praise for their kind act. They told us they already had 20 rescued stray cats at home. I imagined the amount of money they had to spend every month to feed all of them. Yet, they were kind and generous enough to feed one more in the street. "How I wish there are millions more like them," I said. I am sure there are. It's just that in this crowded and noisy world, they are relatively invisible and silent. But what if the majority of the global population can decide that feeding strays is the noblest act anyone do? What if stray animal feeders can become the new kindness champions that society looks up to? It'll take a lot of alchemy work to change the collective mindset, which I think is the hardest to do. But if someone had changed people's worldview on how the universe worked, so can we change modern minds about something so simple yet so powerful.

All we need is the right leadership.

"The greatest leader is not necessarily the one who does the greatest things. He is the one that gets the people to do the greatest things."

– Ronald Reagan, former US President

CHAPTER 04

New Generation of Leaders

"A genuine leader is not a searcher of consensus but a molder of consensus."

– Martin Luther King Jr, activist and political philosopher

Public perception of leadership is increasingly changing. A lot of scholarly articles have been written about the qualities of a leader that are relevant to the current needs and challenges of today. But if you ask anyone, they will tell you more about what they don't want of a leader or leadership style. Leaders and leadership are often talked about in the same breath as politicians and politics. Politics can be a brutal place where politicians often resort to doing anything to survive and cling to power and position. The public is turned off by this. They feel disgusted. Some politicians I know have admittedly told me that in the political arena, there are no real friends nor enemies. In other words, politics, based on their statement, is a place for opportunists, not true leaders. What many people can't understand is that in every election, they continue to vote for individuals with such character to power. Those who make better leaders are nowhere to be found. One aspiring politician I know and who many believed would make a good and honest representative of the community, became so disillusioned with the system that she openly said, "I don't need politics to earn a living."

A leader does not necessarily have to be a politician. He or she can be a captain of an industry or a next-generation entrepreneur. However, there is another type of leader. They are known as cultural leaders. Culture and leadership are powerful forces for growth and change. There are many ways to define a cultural leader; they are creative, innovative, artistic, and always looking to foster expression and social interaction within society. They are also defined as individuals who can guide with a clear vision and connect meaningfully with others. But at the core, I see them as empaths. An empath is a person who is highly attuned to the feelings and emotions of others around them. In a world that is increasingly hurting today; where more and more people are struggling in life, leaders with an attentive ear, a compassionate heart and hunger for change are the ones who deserve to be in power. With power, they will change the world.

We often find people who possess the qualities of a cultural and empathetic leadership in the realm of the arts. For example, the Irish singer and lead vocalist of rock band U2, Bono, used his huge popularity to promote the ONE campaign to fight extreme poverty which helped raise more than $30 billion in funding. The British rock band, Coldplay, has been a huge promoter of environmental sustainability awareness when they pledged in 2022 to reduce their carbon emissions from show production, freight, band and crew travel by "at least 50%" for the Music of the Spheres world tour. The band announced in June 2024 that they had surpassed the figure at 59% compared with their previous world tour. This was achieved with the help of their fans. In a statement on their website, the band thanked "Everyone who's arrived by foot, bike, ride, share or public transport; everyone who's come with refillable water bottles or returned their LED wristband for recycling; and everyone who's bought a ticket, which means you've already planted one of seven million trees so far." It takes a kind-hearted person to make huge commitment toward making a difference to people's lives, be it by addressing poverty or making the planet a safer and healthier place.

Arts and culture can give us a deeper insight into how we form connections and how we relate to the world and help us envision leadership styles that are empathetic and nurturing. This is the type of leadership and stewardship that is more appealing to the present and future generations. You may be this type of a leader; someone who thinks differently. A leader who heals, explores, creates and inspires others. A person who is crazy enough to think he can change the world. And people who think they can change the world are the ones who do.

In her article 'Why Our World Needs a New Leader', Hillary Pennington, the Executive Vice President of Programs for Ford Foundation writes: "To build a future that's truly equitable in a time like this requires a particular kind of leader. Leaders grounded in the issues and deeply aware of the systems and structures at play. Leaders who are unafraid to navigate the unknown in a rapidly evolving world and have the tenacity to forge ahead even when they don't have the answers, seeking solutions from different people, places and cultures. Leaders who have committed to something bigger than themselves – a just, more inclusive world where every person can live with dignity and opportunity – and who have the courage to make it a reality."

Since the most important attribute of a leader is to care, it is important for people to make sure that we select the right ones. Other than being competent in doing their job, the people expect them to be guided by kindness.

"Things will only improve when the people – all of us – say to the authorities, 'I will hold you responsible.' We should all be showing up at city hall council meetings, lighting up every community with activism and mobilization."

– Erin Brockovich, paralegal, consumer advocate, and environmental activist

4.1 Voting Power

"The ballot is stronger than the bullet."

– Abraham Lincoln,
former US President

"Voting is Still One of Our Most Powerful Tools For Change", reads the heading of an article by John Freeman, author and editor of Freeman's. However, we all can agree with him that even though we know that the voting process is not entirely fair, it is the best system we have so far for the voice of the masses to be heard.

For kindness to be a norm in the world, people must be ready to give it a vote, and this means putting the right leaders in positions of power to make high level decisions. With due respect to politics, it is undoubtedly complex, and many people find it difficult to grasp the script of the drama. In extreme circumstances, people have lost their lives because of politics. Despite the complexities, its life clings to one thing: a vote, and it's in our hands. "A voter is a mighty thing; a single voter has decided elections. A single voter has led to sweeping social change. A single vote, in, say, a justice system ruling, has led to the overturning of some of the worst and most discriminating practices in many of our societies," adds Freeman.

There is a meme showing a wolf promising a flock of sheep he would turn vegetarian if they voted for him. We all know that will never happen. Voters everywhere are fed-up with leaders who always make empty promises. But often they didn't have a choice of the right candidates because these individuals were selected by their parties. To give the people the power to choose, a former politician friend of mine told me of his plan to create a platform where anyone can propose names of people who they think possess the right qualities to be elected and represent them.

Although in some countries, independents have been on the rise as people move away from party politics, my friend knew it wasn't going to be easy for him to realise his idea in a society so used to hyper-partisan politics. "People tell me that they've lost trust in the political parties. At the same time, they're stuck with the idea that voting for a political party is the only way to form the government. People are not comfortable about change."

I believe, however, that change is inevitable. People are tired of playing the game where they throw a handful of sticky toys against the wall and see which ones will stick. When we create a kinder world, power will be in the safe hands of the right leaders.

"Be a warrior when it comes to delivering on your ambitions. And a saint when it comes to treating people with respect, modeling generosity, and showing up with outright love."

– Robin Sharma, writer

CHAPTER 05

Show Up and Stand Up

"Perseverance doesn't mean winning and losing. Perseverance means showing up and rising to the occasion and performing."

– Michael Chiesa, professional mixed martial artist

It is also important to understand that being kind is not just about being nice. It must be a source of motivation to bring about a systemic change in the world. This means a system overhaul to create a lasting difference. This typically involves changing policies, power structures and mindsets within the complex interdependent social system. No one says this will be easy but if more people show up and take a stand, there will always be a realistic chance to push the power of kindness as a strategy to change the world.

Robyne Hanley-Dafoe, a resiliency and wellness scholar and speaker and the award-winning author of Calm Within the Storm: A Pathway to Everyday Resiliency and Stress Wisely: How To Be Well in An Unwell World. She writes, "Kindness is about showing up in the world with compassion and acting for the greater good of all. While being nice is about being polite, pleasant, and agreeable and doing what we think we should, kindness goes a step beyond." She continues with a quote: "Kindness begins with the understanding that we all struggle."

We don't need more evidence to show how painful our life's struggles are. We are struggling even to meet the basics like food and shelter. It looks like for the majority of us, to exist on this planet we must pay a high price that keeps getting higher. A friend had once complained that he had to pay 0.30 cents more just to pee in a public toilet. "It's not only what we put into our mouth costs more these days, but also what we discharge. Who is profiting? It's absurd."

But the thing is, people haven't shown up and risen up enough to raise a collective awareness of what is actually going on in the world. I sometimes wonder if social movements around the world are no longer listening to the unspoken voices of the people or capturing their imagination. When asked for her thoughts about what makes a social movement prosper, Hahrie Han, a Political Science professor at Johns Hopkins University and author of several books on social movements said: "First, a lot of social movements mistake attention for power. We live in an attention economy. But attention doesn't necessarily mean that you can actually make the change that you want."

"The second thing is a lot of social movements mistake mobilising for organising. So, mobilising is about trying to essentially harness people's outrage. And because of all the tools that we have with new technologies, it's easier than ever before to phrase just the right question to get lots of millions of people who are really angry about something to come out and take action. Organising, on the other hand, is about actually transforming people's capabilities to turn people who are just outraged into people who are actually working with each other to create the kind of flexibility and strategic capacity they need to make the change that they want."

Around the world, there are many movements that are committed to spreading kindness and pushing it to be the norm. One of them is the World Kindness Movement (WKM), whose work gives us an idea of how powerful the concept of kindness is. It started back in 1997 when Japan brought together like-minded kindness organisations from all over the world for the first time to a conference in Tokyo. There, the formation of the World Kindness Movement (WKM) was crystallised. Recognised as "the peak global body for kindness", it serves as a platform for collaboration and sharing. WKM's mission is to inspire individuals towards greater kindness by connecting nations to create a kinder world. Members of the movement include over 27 nations with representatives from Australia, Brazil, Canada, China, France, India, Italy, Japan, Liberia, Malaysia, Mexico, Nepal, Netherlands, New Zealand, Nigeria, Oman, Pakistan, Romania, Scotland, South Africa, South Korea, Switzerland, Thailand, United

Arab Emirates, Uganda, Ukraine, United Kingdom, the USA and Zimbabwe.

In 1998, WKM introduced World Kindness Day, which is observed every year on November 13. What all this means is that the concept of kindness has reached a high level with the participation of key stakeholders from all countries. The rest of the world, especially visionary leaders of kindness, should build on this to make kindness a lot more mainstream.

Alongside organisations and movements, there are many individuals and thought leaders who have made it their mission to make this world kinder. We do in fact have the numbers of kindness armies already fighting on the frontlines. But we need new recruits to raise a global campaign for kindness as a new norm or a gold standard in all social systems and structures. To do this takes a lot of organising work.

"Learn from the people
Plan with the people
Begin with what they have
Build on what they know
Of the best leaders
When the task is accomplished
The people all remark
We have done it ourselves."

– Lao-Tzu, Tao Te Ching

CHAPTER 06

Community Organising Lessons from Indigenous Peoples

"Humankind has not woven the web of life. We are but one thread within it. Whatever we do to the web, we do to ourselves. All things are bound together. All things connect."

– Chief Seattle, Duwamish

The Indigenous Peoples' traditional worldview is that everything in life is interconnected. In 2006, I took leave from my job as a journalist to be involved in the Indigenous Peoples movement in Sabah, Malaysia. My role was to help the local communities tell their stories; all the struggles they were facing, their traditional knowledge and practices that may offer solutions to the world's biggest problems and their innovations as well as spirituality to mainstream society.

I volunteered in a local community-based organisation called Pacos Trust. On my first day stepping into their small office, the first sign I saw on the wall was 'Community

Organising', which was one of its main work programmes. The programme coordinator later explained to me that community organising was the heart of the movement. The 24-month programme provides technical and practical training for community organisers. The goal is to build and enhance their capacity to address issues faced by their respective community, and by the Indigenous Peoples collectively.

There are nearly half a billion Indigenous Peoples in the world living across 90 countries. They make up a small percentage of the world's population, but account for 15 per cent of the poorest. They are the most diverse peoples in the world. They speak an overwhelming majority of the world's estimated 7,000 languages and represent 5,000 different cultures. They inherit and still practice their unique cultures and ways of relating to people and the environment. Their social, cultural, economic and political characteristics are distinct from those of the dominant societies in which they live.

Despite their cultural differences, indigenous peoples from around the world share common problems related to the protection of their rights as distinct peoples. They also share a common history of colonization, conquest or occupation that goes back for centuries. Their histories of resistance are well documented. Some states recognise the sovereignty of indigenous peoples. This is evident by hundreds of treaties signed between them and governments of some countries. Treaties however meant nothing if they were not honoured and when the indigenous peoples saw this happening countless of times, they started organising themselves globally to get international attention to their issues.

The Indigenous Peoples global activism traces its beginnings way back to 1923, when Cayuga Chief Deskaheh, the representative of the Six Nations of the Iroquois travelled to Geneva, to the League of Nations, to plead for the cause of his people. He wanted to obtain international recognition of the Haudenosaunee Confederacy (historically known as the Six Nations of the Iroquois Confederacy, composed of the Mohawk, Oneida, Onondaga, Cayuga, Seneca, and Tuscarora Nations) as a sovereign Indigenous Nation governed by a hereditary council of chiefs.

He waited a whole year to obtain recognition from the League but was not received and returned home to North America. Although he was not granted an audience by the League, he did sustain a remarkably successful PR campaign in Europe, where he found a much more receptive audience in the media and general public than he did amongst the delegations in the League.

A similar journey was made the following year by Maori religious leader W.T. Rātana to protest at the breakdown of the Treaty of Waitangi, concluded in 1840 between representatives of the British Crown and Maori chiefs in New Zealand, a treaty that gave Maori ownership of their lands. In 1924 Rātana took a petition to London, signed by more than 30,000 Māori. They called for the return of confiscated lands, and implementation of the Treaty. He was not allowed to speak with King George V. A member of the group also tried and failed to present the petition to the League of Nations in Geneva. But Rātana's actions did help persuade the New Zealand government, in 1926, to set up a commission of inquiry (the Sim Commission). It was to investigate land confiscation, and it later upheld many Māori grievances over land.

The decolonization era in the 1960s and 1970s saw the establishment of indigenous peoples' organizations around the world at national and international levels. The issues that fuelled the movement ranged from broken treaties and loss of land to discrimination, marginalization, conflict and gross violations of human rights, including massacres. Although most of the activities of the nascent international indigenous movement took place outside the environs of the United Nations, indigenous peoples' voices were at last being heard, and the UN was finally willing to listen to these voices.

The impact of Pacos Trust's Community Organising programme is evident by the establishment of hundreds of grassroots people's organisations. Many of them are situated deep in the rural areas and are desperately defending their traditional territories, knowledge and lifestyle.

During the two years I was with the organisation, I had the opportunity to attend international meetings where I met Indigenous Peoples representatives from many countries. Each of the countries had quite a number of organisations that were strongly rooted in hundreds of communities they represented. We formed not just working relationship but long-lasting friendships. It was from these interactions that I understood how widely connected the global Indigenous People's movement is around the world. They were not just wide but deep. And because they are strongly organised, they have access to intervene in high-level decision-making processes such as in the United Nations. They are a force that world leaders can't ignore.

On August 1, 2016, Taiwan President Tsai Ing-wen officially apologised to the island's Indigenous Peoples on behalf of the government for centuries of mistreatment. She was the first leader to have ever done so. "For the past 400 years, each regime that came to Taiwan has brutally violated Indigenous Peoples' existing rights through military might and land looting," she reportedly said. I believe this historic moment was the result of strong community organising and advocacy from the country's 5 million minority indigenous population.

A global kindness movement may draw lessons from the Indigenous Peoples' journey in building a global network and presence. They can start building solidarity among existing movements, expand wider and build depth through the creation of grassroots champions. Together, they can campaign for kindness to be made a policy in governance or develop solutions to some of the world's biggest challenges.

"Life is the story you tell yourself. But how you tell that story – are you a hero, victim, lover, warrior, caretaker, believer – matters a great deal. How you adapt that story – how you revise, rethink and rewrite your personal narrative as things change, lurch, or go wrong in your life – matters even more."

– Bruce Feiler, writer

CHAPTER 07

Do You Hear the Crickets or the Coins?

"We only see what we want to see; we only hear what we want to hear. Our belief system is just like a mirror that only shows us what we believe."

– Don Miguel Ruiz, Mexican author

Some may say that your desire and passion to change the world is just a naive and hopeful optimism; that the world's problems are too big for any single person to solve. Whether you believe you can change the world or not depends on your belief and the stories you tell yourself. Henry Ford says, "If you think you can or you think you can't, you're right,". I was talking with a friend about the need for the common people to be aware of the dangerous and damaging trends in the world, and how the power of kindness could disrupt them. He didn't believe it was possible and convincingly gave all the reasons to support his conviction. He said it was too high an ideal for anyone to reach, let alone live up to. I felt defeated because I knew it was not a single person's opinion. Millions more would think the same way.

But I quickly switched back to optimism with the belief that millions, if not billions, of people were willing to make change work; that remaining in the status quo would be suicidal. It all depends on what is important to us.

To drive this point, there's a story about an indigenous person and his friend who were in downtown New York City, walking near Times Square in Manhattan. The streets were filled people. Cars were honking their horns, taxicabs were squealing around corners, sirens were wailing, and the sounds of the city were almost deafening. Suddenly, the Native American said, "I hear a cricket." His friend said. "What? You must be crazy. You couldn't possibly hear a cricket in all this noise!"

"No, I'm sure of it," the Native American said, "I heard a cricket."

"That's crazy," said the friend.

The Native American listened carefully for a moment, and then walked across the street to a big cement planter where some shrubs were growing. He looked into the bushes, beneath the branches, and sure enough, he located a small cricket. His friend was utterly amazed.

"That's incredible," said his friend. "You must have super-human ears!"

"No," said the Native American. "My ears are no different from yours. It all depends on what you're listening for."

"But that can't be!" said the friend. "I could never hear a cricket in this noise."

"Yes, it's true," came the reply. "It depends on what is really important to you. Here, let me show you."

He reached into his pocket, pulled out a few coins, and discreetly dropped them on the sidewalk. And then, with the noise of the crowded street still blaring in their ears, they noticed every person within twenty feet turned and looked to see if the money that tinkled on the pavement was theirs.

"See what I mean?" asked the Native American. "It all depends on what's important to you.

"All stories have a curious, even dangerous power. They are manifestations of truth – yours and mine. And truth is all at once the most wonderful yet terrifying thing in the world, which makes it nearly impossible to handle. It is such a great responsibility that it's best not to tell a story at all unless you know you can do it right. You must be very careful, or without knowing it you can change the world."

– Vera Nazarian, Dreams of The Compass Rose

CHAPTER 08

Take Control of Your Own Story

"The most powerful words in English are, "Tell me a story"."

– Pat Conroy, My Reading Life

In a world where opinions of others are paraded as facts, it is important that we take control of our own story, our own truth. If we believe that we can collectively work toward building a global agenda of kindness to disrupt power systems, structures and mindsets that don't serve us, then this is the narrative we must sell to the collective human consciousness. Leaders of kindness can learn a lot from the world's most powerful media organisations in selling an opinion or controlling a narrative.

My former boss had called me one day and excitedly told me about his plan to take over a defunct local newspaper. I was then working as a journalist for a company owned by his family that owned the largest English newspaper in East Malaysia. He had been wanting to start his own newspaper business and invited me to build it with him. Being a black sheep in the family, he had his own idea about how we, as news people, should be telling stories to the public. I was caught unprepared when he told me the new name of the new newspaper. "Happy," he said. What? No way! I objected because the name didn't sound newspaper-like to me at all. To me, traditional newspapers normally have 'Post' or 'Times' or 'Express' in their names.

"Why not?" he said. "We want people to be reading happy stories first thing in the morning."

Most news outlets lead with bad news, from tragedies, crimes, scandals to corruptions. You may have ever wondered why breaking news is mostly about things that are happening around the world. It causes us to operate our daily life on a "bad news" mode. A mind that eats bad news for breakfast will go about the rest of the day with bad news in mind. It's like a mind programmed for bad things to happen. It is depressing and unhealthy. Whereas stories about people's acts of kindness to one another or to animals may either be 'killed' by editors or put deep in the inside pages as human interest. There is an old media adage "If it bleeds it leads." Psychologists call it "negativity bias", our collective hunger to hear, and remember bad news that makes us feel depressed and angry.

I came across one quote said to be from Andrew Carnegie, notably one of the richest Americans in history: "If the newspapers begin to publish stories about wars, and the people begin to think and talk of war in their daily conversations, they soon find themselves at war. People get that which their minds dwell upon, and this applies to a group or community or a nation of people. The same as to an individual." My ex-boss had wanted to change this. He wanted to change the stories people tell themselves.

My ex-boss was not just a black sheep in his family. He was different from other people I know. As a friend, he had often shared his worldview with me, and it was one that was beautiful, happy, peaceful, kind and non-judgmental. It's a world seen through the eyes of a child. He understood the power of the media as the controller of narratives. Owning a newspaper would put him in the position of power and influence to be the voice that speaks of the purest desires of the human soul.

Gretchen Busl, a narrative scholar who studied how stories work and affect people's perceptions, had elaborated on the role they play in shaping people's values and belief systems. She asked the audience during her talk on TEDx to examine the narratives they were being presented every day and be deliberate in knowing who was framing the story. "Whoever controls the narratives has the power. So, take control of your story," she said.

“Follow the path of the unsafe, independent thinker. Expose your ideas to the danger of controversy. Speak your mind and fear less the label of ‘crackpot’ than the stigma of conformity.”

– Thomas J. Watson, Chairman and CEO of IBM

CHAPTER 09

We are Wired to Conform

Don't follow the crowd, let the crowd follow you. - Margaret Thatcher,

– former British Prime Minister

People who dream of changing the world are usually the ones who understand the pain and struggles. They see how things have not been going in the right direction. These people include you and I who make up the majority of the world's population; we who are always at the receiving end of whatever decisions made and directions set by the powerful minority.

Our challenge is to unite ourselves so we can create an influence. In the science of conformity, group size matters. You may have watched videos of social experiments being conducted to show proof of this. In the videos, an unsuspecting individual gets into the elevator, presses the button and stands facing the door (as anyone would do without thinking). Then a group of people who are part of the experiment comes in and all of them stand facing the rear. Some of the members of the group apply peer pressure on the subject by staring at her, making her feel uncomfortable and obviously wondering why everyone is facing the rear. It doesn't take long before she turns to face the same direction as the rest.

I thought some of the videos were very funny. One that I watched recently showed two men in the elevator. One of them is the subject of the experiment, while the other is an actor. Then enters a man dressed like a soldier and in a loud voice, announces the arrival of a couple who acted as a king and his consort. The other actor in the elevator bows to the "majesties" as the confused subject watches. Feeling pressured when seeing everyone is staring at him, he takes a bow as well.

The experiment owes to the work of Polish-American Gestalt psychologist and pioneer in social psychology, Solomon Asch, known today as the Asch conformity experiments. They were a series of groundbreaking psychological experiments conducted by him in the 1950s. The experiments revealed the degree to which a person's own opinions are influenced by those of a group. He found that people were willing to ignore reality and give an incorrect answer in order to conform to the rest of the group. "The pressure to conform is so powerful that we are often willing to suppress our own perceptions and judgments in order to gain the acceptance and approval of others," says one of his famous quotes.

This speaks true to all of us. How many times have we hidden our truth and our beliefs just to conform to the majority, even though we know they were wrong.

"Nothing in the world is worth having or worth doing unless it means effort, pain, difficulty...I have never in my life envied a human being who led an easy life."

– Theodore Roosevelt, former US President

CHAPTER 10

Nobody Says It's Easy

"It takes courage to be kind."

– Maya Angelou, memoirist, poet and civil rights activist

Amazon founder Jeff Bezos once recounted a story about how he, as a child, was excellent in math and would find every opportunity to show off his prowess with numbers. One day, while sitting in the back of his grandparents' car, he heard an advert on the radio, which said that smoking takes minutes off a smoker's total lifespan. His grandmother was a smoker, so he decided to calculate the number of years she had taken off her life thus far.

"I estimated the number of cigarettes per day, estimated the number of puffs per cigarette and so on," Bezos told the graduating class at Princeton University.

"When I was satisfied...I poked my head into the front of the car, tapped my grandmother on the shoulder and proudly proclaimed, "At two minutes per puff, you've taken nine years off your life!" he explained. His grandmother was upset and cried.

His grandfather then pulled him aside and calmly told him, “Jeff, one day you’ll understand that it’s harder to be kind than clever.”

But here’s the irony. We are living in a world where we have access to an unlimited source of information, yet we are not getting any clever, let alone any wiser. Come to think of it, Artificial Intelligence is increasingly doing all the thinking for us which to me is a tragedy. When we let it do most of that work, we pass on the opportunity to exercise important parts of our brains. It’s a polite way of explaining what stupidity is.

To be clever is to be kind, and vice versa. Besides, kindness is the factory setting in all of us and it’s the cleverest choice we can make to save us from further ruins.

"The tragedy of life is often not in our failure, but rather in our complacency; not in our doing too much, but rather in our doing too little; not in our living above our ability, but rather in our living below our capacities."

– Benjamin E. Mays, educator

CHAPTER 11

Do You Sense It?

"What you know you can't explain, but you feel it. You've felt it your entire life, that there's something wrong with the world. You don't know what it is, but it's there, like a splinter in your mind, driving you mad."

– Morpheus, Matrix-Code

Here's a fable you may have read before: If you put a frog directly into boiling water, it will jump right out of the pot. But if you put it in tepid water and turn up the heat slowly, it will stay in the water until it cooks to death.

Are we being slowly "cooked" without realising it?

I don't mean this to be a doomsday message, but many people are increasingly waking up to a world they perceive as wicked and dark. They feel as if the world is holding its breath in anticipation of something bad. This has resulted in a feeling of nervousness in the human collective. People are increasingly wondering what is going on but don't really know what questions to ask, or who to ask. Youtuber Stephen Antonioni asks the same question in his video "Does Anyone Else Feel Like Everything Has

Changed?" that has been viewed by 3.7 million viewers. From his readings of the works of some of the world's brilliant thinkers, Antonioni observes that during period when he was growing up in the 90s people generally had some level of faith in the institutions, God and themselves. And then the internet emerged and exposed our dark side for all to see. "And I've been hard pressed to find a single soul who harbors any amount of faith that we are headed anywhere except in the wrong direction. What is happening to us?" Towards the end, he says, "In many ways, the world is a better place than it was yesterday. Just judging by objective measures. But I can't help shake the feeling that something is off and perhaps terribly so. And therefore, I have to ask the question: Does anyone else feel like everything has changed?"

As a person born in the 60s, I can come up with a long list of changes that have taken place in my life over five decades. But none of the life's changes that I have gone through have raised any serious concern than seeing a child turning violent after her mother took away a tablet from her. I thought such behaviour is unnatural for any 4-year-old child. It was not the only time I saw children reacting in such a manner. My fear is that this might have already become a universal pattern of behaviour among innocent children in the digital age. If this is true, then social media, powered by the internet, has not only exposed our dark side, but distorts the true light of innocence from shining into the early years of a child.

American political scientist, author, and entrepreneur, Ian Bremmer, suggests that we are in the era of digital order. And it is not run by governments but by technology companies. "Technology companies increasingly determine our identities. When I was growing up, it's nature and nurture. I mean, my deep and abiding emotional problems either come from how I was raised or some genetic failure. It could be both. But today, identities are determined by nature and nurture, and algorithm. If you want to challenge the system, you can't just question authority as we were all told when we were growing up. Today, you have to question the algorithm, and that is a staggering amount of power in the hands of these technology companies. What are they going to do with that power?"

He adds: "There is no pause button on these explosive and disruptive technologies. I don't know if you know this. There are over 100 people in the world today with the knowledge and the technology to create a new smallpox virus. Honestly, I don't have answers. But I have a few questions for the people that do. Because these technology companies are not just Fortune 50 and 100 actors. These technology titans are not just men worth 50 or $100 billion or more. They are increasingly the most powerful people on the planet with influence over our futures. And we need to know. Are they going to act accountably as they release new and powerful artificial intelligence?"

Research shows that one of the impacts of screen addiction on children, especially exposure to violent and hate content, is that it desensitizes them to the pain and suffering of others. This is seriously concerning because it can lead to a world where fakeness and unkindness become the norm.

We may choose to ignore all the changes that are taking place in our lives and in the world. But I believe many people are already seeing the dark side of the world and now cannot unsee it. It's the unkind side of it. Unless we start realising the urgent need to take collective action to change the world, we risk getting cooked in boiling water.

"The Age of Aquarius will belong to those who can look at themselves in the mirror and create something beautiful. The Age of Aquarius belongs to these brave romantics."

– Rico Roho, author

CHAPTER 12

The Aquarian Push

"Everything is energy and that's all there is to it. Match the frequency of the reality you want, and you cannot help but get that reality. It can be no other way. This is not philosophy. This is physics."

– Albert Einstein, Physicist

Here is where the logical mind may find a bit difficult to grasp. But what defies logic doesn't mean it's untrue. I believe there has been a major shift happening where we are entering into an era marked by a time when our collective consciousness evolves, leading to a greater focus on spirituality, interconnectedness, and the realization of our shared humanity. It encourages us to think beyond ourselves and work towards a better future for all. And we can already see this happening as more and more people are seeking a deeper understanding of themselves and the universe. Astrologers say this shift is taking place because we are entering (although there's a lot of debate on the actual timing) into the Age of Aquarius.

This age has been the buzz words these days. It catalyses for us the release of old patterns, fears, and limiting beliefs that no longer serve our highest good. By embracing the spiritual opportunities presented during this era, we can evolve into conscious co-creators, actively participating in the realization of a more enlightened and compassionate world.

It is no surprise that there has been a significant increase in the interest and practice of spirituality all around the world. By spirituality, I don't mean religion because like politics, it can be divisive. People with broader spiritual perspectives are becoming more aware of their abilities to find a sense of wholeness within. This involves the ability to be kind to themselves as the first condition before they can be genuinely kind to others. This is very important in the work of building a kinder world. Spiritual and thought leaders are increasingly being listened to because more people are putting value in inner work. They're allowing the alchemist within them to do the work because they have faith that the result is going to be 'shining pure gold'.

Together with artists, kindness activists, entrepreneurs, philosophers, mystics, healers, empaths, writers, they are rising as powerful agents of change. Other key traits associated with this new era include innovation and originality, and so, we can expect to witness significant advancements in science, technology, and societal progress.

This powerful astrological shift creates a fertile ground for kindness to become a force for change and be the norm. However, to achieve this it is important to get as many like-minded leaders on the same page; be as one huge army of kindness. This is the way forward. As we are influenced by the powerful force of the mighty shift, I believe it is a matter of time when all of them will come together in support of one another toward a shared goal. When that happens, it'll be the game-changer.

"To believe a business impossible is the way to make it so. How many feasible projects have miscarried through despondency and been strangled in their birth by a cowardly imagination."

– Jeremy Collier, theologian

CHAPTER 13

The Alchemical Process of Making Kindness a Force to Catalyse Global Change

"There is only one way to learn...It's through action. Everything you need to know you have learned through your journey."

– Paolo Coelho, author 'The Alchemist'

Gold has so captured the human imagination that alchemists from around the world were for centuries obsessed with the transformation of base metals, especially lead, into it. Using a mythical substance called the "philosopher's stone", they set out to accomplish the task but without success. Their failures led them to be looked down on as nothing more than pseudoscientific charlatans. But today, nuclear physicists routinely transform one element to another. So, the alchemists hundreds of years ago were truly onto something big. And they were indeed for their practice of alchemy paved the way for modern chemistry.

In this book, I've explained the philosophical concepts of kindness as a powerful force for global change. I've put up a case that a new world order must be built on the fundamental values of kindness, empathy and compassion; and that these are not just some nice feelings but policies that govern all social systems and power structures.

In this chapter, I unpack some of the steps on how the concepts may be brought down to Earth into actionable goals.

13.1 Break Down Old Beliefs

To build something new, the old must be destroyed.

In the first chapter of the book, I used the example of the now-adult viewers of the popular children's educational television series, Blue's Clues, to explain about the silent pain and suffering most people were going through every day in the world. No one deserves to live a life like this but to believe that we can change it takes a lot of 'burning away' of everything that is no longer serving us. The first thing that must burn is the old belief that we are powerless to change the world.

It is not easy to change a deeply rooted belief that we have been holding on to for most of our lives. One powerful way to weaken its power is by replacing it with a new belief. We can do this by telling ourselves that it is possible to transform our lives and the world. Then all we need to do is to repeat this mantra over and over until it takes root in our consciousness. This is a real phenomenon that is well established and extensively studied in cognitive science. It is known as the illusory truth effect. Hearing or reading a claim repeatedly makes us more likely to think it is true. In the same manner, if we repeat a lie often enough, it could become the truth.

Being aware of this phenomenon can be a low-hanging fruit for people who have been devoting their lives to making this world a better place. This is important because it is always easy to feel defeated. Constant mind programming is the fuel to burn the fire.

13.2 Connect and Participate

It takes great vision and character for anyone to aim at changing the world. Not everyone is called for this task. But many have answered the call, and we can all correctly guess there are many of them. Perhaps in the millions.

Around the world, there are many movements that are promoting kindness as a norm. Some of them have been around for a long time. It will greatly help amplify their message and work when more people give them their support. Some movements that I've come across welcome anyone to be a member. They are also open to new ideas on how to push the kindness agenda forward. When like-minded people come together, it creates a sense of shared identity and purpose. This is power.

It doesn't always have to be a serious change-the-world mission. It may just be a fun experience of connecting with people from around the world who value kindness. Like many people, I've always been a football fan since I was a young boy. To me, no other sport has fans around the world that follow their favourite football teams like they do with religion. While we would always avoid running into a friend, or worse a stranger, who is wearing the exact same shirt that we are wearing, football fans don't find a moment of jersey 'accident' embarrassing at all. I've experienced such moments many times. Instead of feeling awkward, I felt connected with the person wearing the same kit. The feeling of unity and solidarity is more intense when you sit in a stadium with thousands of fans, all wearing the same colours. You feel dissolved in the moment. Your team's purpose to win the match becomes yours, too.

The global kindness movements may still be far from being able to build an army of followers like football teams. But if they remain persistent in selling their stories to the world, and doing it repeatedly, sooner or later they will grow in numbers. We are, after all, a storytelling species. We are wired that way.

13.3 Sell the Kindness Story

Some of the world's biggest brands have spent a huge amount of money on creating and selling their stories. They don't directly sell their products but invest heavily on the power of storytelling. Through their stories, they sell universal values such as perseverance, excellence or authenticity.

Kindness movement leaders and changemakers may copy this strategy to sell the idea of kindness as the new norm to the masses. This can be fun, and I believe the sky is the limit when it comes to developing creative project ideas on ways to connect the story of their vision and dream consumers around the world.

I've been a collector of memes that tell the story of kindness. One of my many collections is a picture showing a man covering a stray dog from the rain with an umbrella. Below the picture is a caption that reads, *Why Is This Not Mainstream?* The social media is flooded with memes and videos on kindness, compassion and empathy, which is a positive sign. I salute the individuals and groups who created these contents and put them out to the world. However, it will take some deep thinking and strategizing on how to make them mainstream. I think to achieve this, calls for teamwork. We can never know that the next great idea might come from the next person we meet. This again goes back to the need to stay connected with like-minded souls as I've mentioned earlier.

13.4 Everything Starts with an idea

Actor and comedian, Robin Williams, once said, "No matter what people tell you, words and ideas can change the world." We can all agree that everything starts with an idea. One simple idea may have the power to change the world. To generate a great idea, we need to be creative. We must be willing to abandon traditional ways of looking at things.

The idea or solution may be irrational at first but over time, it will become rational.

The belief that the collective force of kindness can change the world is a very big idea. Too big until some of my friends thought it was not possible to realise. But history has taught us that some of the ideas that were put out centuries or decades ago have changed the world. The Ancient Greek philosopher, Plato, proposed a dualistic view of human nature. This perspective sees the human person as composed of two fundamentally different elements: the soul (or spirit) and the body. For Plato, the soul is immortal, rational, and the essence of one's identity, while the body is temporary, irrational, and often an obstacle to the soul's desires. He believes that for humans to flourish, the way to achieve it is through philosophy, which during his time was a relatively new discipline. He equates human happiness with the inner harmony of the human soul. His idea was later developed by the Christians into our 'conscience' which was a hugely important move in the history of Western ethics and religion.

Another revolutionary idea, which is closer to our time, comes from Albert Einstein's Theory of Relativity which at first sight didn't seem like an idea that would transform the world because it was a strange theory. It sounds very esoteric. But it's the foundation of every modern theory we have on the way the world works, whether it's electricity and magnetism or silicon chips or transistors. All these theories are based on relativity. If Einstein hadn't thought of the theory, we could not have the modern view of the world that we have today.

So, I believe there is nothing to lose in pursuing a big idea. Who knows it will be the next big thing that will change everything.

13.5 Pilot a Kindness Landscape

In 2023, I was working on a project for a foreign organisation on sustainable oil palm in a small east coast district in Sabah, on the Island of Borneo. The organisation's mission was to raise the bar for sustainable production, environmental protection and social inclusion through what is called a landscape approach.

Landscape approaches apply a broad range of tried and tested strategies and methods for the sustainable management of natural resources. Also known as a jurisdictional or integrated landscape approach, it is a framework for inclusive and multi sectoral land use management and territorial development. This approach means bringing together groups of producers, companies, government and civil society to improve sustainability in the district.

My task was to develop a four-year roadmap and bring all the stakeholders together on a common mission to achieve the highest standards of sustainability in the district landscape. The stakeholders were from the local government, government agencies, private companies, civil society, producers, NGOs, and smallholders. Part of the roadmap was to integrate all the stakeholders into the inclusive governance structure for the district.

I think a similar project could be implemented anywhere in the world for kindness. I call it a Kindness Landscape Approach. The idea behind this is that all life forms – humans, animals and nature – within a particular landscape are interconnected and this interconnection could be enhanced through acts of kindness. Let me take one example from the work I did to explain what I mean by acts of kindness in this context. The landscape where I was working had been facing the problem of human and wildlife conflict. This happened because most of the lands in the district have been used for agriculture, leaving only pockets of natural forests for wildlife to roam in search of food. Occasionally, wildlife like elephants and Orangutans would encroach into agriculture lands either to find food to eat or to cross to the other patch of forest. To ensure that humans and wildlife could co-exist, the project identified a few solutions one of which was to create a wildlife corridor. The idea was to plant trees along the corridor which would eventually connect some of the identified pockets of forest. This would enable the animals to move about freely and safely while at the same time reduce incidents of wildlife encroachment into agriculture lands. This goal was to be achieved through collaborations among various stakeholders in the landscape. So, how is this an act of kindness you might ask? I believe in this context kindness is served when humans respect the place and purpose of animals on the planet. If we think about it, animals are increasingly living under the threat of losing their natural habitat as humans continue to grab more lands in the name of development.

There are today many ongoing projects by NGOs, communities and authorities that are trying to tackle issues like this in many parts of the world. We always read about some of these projects as wildlife or biodiversity protection or inclusion. However, I think it would be great if somewhere in the main title, the word kindness is used. It would help create greater awareness of the importance and urgency of being a kind soul on this interconnected planet.

Piloting a project like this within the boundaries of a landscape will make it easier for stakeholders to push the kindness agenda to the government and authorities in the hope that sound kindness-driven policies could be drafted and implemented. For instance, recently a beloved stray dog named Kopi, who had captured hearts nationwide in Malaysia, was killed in an alleged culling operation. The incident sparked outrage with animal rights groups in the country demanding legal action against a local council. An Instagram post showed the final moments of the whimpering dog on the road as she was consoled by a passer-by. Social media was flooded with reactions from the public, condemning the cruelty and demanding justice for Kopi. Killing of stray animals should never be a solution.

In fact, it must never be allowed. Through a Kindness Landscape Approach, stakeholders might work together, in the name of kindness for animals who are also part of life within the landscape, to come up with a better solution. They might also want to enforce strong policies to protect the existence of all life forms in the landscape, not just humans.

Stakeholders may include local government and authorities, schools, community-based associations, clubs, social and environmental NGOs, animal rights groups, stray animal feeders and individuals. They will convene from time to time to set goals and targets, plan activities, explore fundraising opportunities as well as to co-develop ideas on making kindness the norm in the landscape.

If my proposed pilot Kindness Landscape Approach project idea could be implemented and proven successful, I believe in time it will be replicated in many places around the world. When this happens, the world will witness a big coalition of kind landscapes powerful enough to push for a global transformation. This has been my dream.

“The most authentic thing about us is our capacity to create, to overcome, to endure, to transform, to love and to be greater than our suffering.”

– Ben Okri, Poet and Novelist

CHAPTER 14

Kindness in the Worst Moment of Humanity

"The most beautiful people we have known are those who have known defeat, known suffering, known struggle, known loss, and have found their way out of those depths."

– Elisabeth Kubler-Ross, Psychiatrist

Many of you might be familiar with the remarkable event during the First World War. It came to be called the Christmas Truce. It happened on Christmas Eve in 1914 in the muddy trenches on the Western Front. Thousands of British, Belgian and French soldiers put down their rifles, stepped out of their trenches and spent Christmas mingling with their German enemies. The event has been seen as a kind of miracle, a rare moment of peace just a few months into a war that would eventually claim over 15 million lives.

A.J. Baime & Volker Janssen wrote beautifully about the miraculous event on the HISTORY website. Here's part of the article:

On Christmas Eve 1914, in the dank, muddy trenches on the Western Front of the First World War, a remarkable thing happened.

It came to be called the Christmas Truce. And it remains one of the most storied and strangest moments of the Great War—or of any war in history.

British machine gunner Bruce Bairnsfather, later a prominent cartoonist, wrote about it in his memoirs. Like most of his fellow infantrymen of the 1st Battalion of the Royal Warwickshire Regiment, he was spending the holiday eve shivering in the muck, trying to keep warm. He had spent a good part of the past few months fighting the Germans. And now, in a part of Belgium called Bois de Ploegsteert, he was crouched in a trench that stretched just three feet deep by three feet wide, his days and nights marked by an endless cycle of sleeplessness and fear, stale biscuits and cigarettes too wet to light.

"Here I was, in this horrible clay cavity," Bairnsfather wrote, "...miles and miles from home. Cold, wet through and covered with mud." There didn't "seem the slightest chance of leaving—except in an ambulance."

At about 10 p.m., Bairnsfather noticed a noise. "I listened," he recalled. "Away across the field, among the dark shadows beyond, I could hear the murmur of voices." He turned to a fellow soldier in his trench and said, "Do you hear the Boches [Germans] kicking up that racket over there?"

"Yes," came the reply. "They've been at it some time!"

The Germans were singing carols, as it was Christmas Eve. In the darkness, some of the British soldiers began to sing back. "Suddenly," Bairnsfather recalled, "we heard a confused shouting from the other side. We all stopped to listen. The shout came again." The voice was from an enemy soldier, speaking in English with a strong German accent. He was saying, "Come over here."

One of the British sergeants answered: "You come half-way. I come half-way."

What happened next would, in the years to come, stun the world and make history. Enemy soldiers began to climb nervously out of their trenches, and to meet in the barbed-wire-filled "No Man's Land" that separated the armies. Normally, the British and Germans communicated across No Man's Land with streaking bullets, with only occasional gentlemanly allowances to collect the dead unmolested. But now, there were handshakes and words of kindness. The soldiers traded songs, tobacco and wine, joining in a spontaneous holiday party in the cold night.

Bairnsfather could not believe his eyes. "Here they were—the actual, practical soldiers of the German army. There was not an atom of hate on either side."

And it wasn't confined to that one battlefield. Starting on Christmas Eve, small pockets of French, German, Belgian and British troops held impromptu cease-fires across the

Western Front, with reports of some on the Eastern Front as well. Some accounts suggest a few of these unofficial truces remained in effect for days.

For those who participated, it was surely a welcome break from the hell they had been enduring. When the war had begun just six months earlier, most soldiers figured it would be over quickly and they'd be home with their families in time for the holidays. Not only would the war drag on for four more years, but it would prove to be the bloodiest conflict ever up to that time. The Industrial Revolution had made it possible to mass-produce new and devastating tools for killing—among them fleets of airplanes and guns that could fire hundreds of rounds per minute. And bad news on both sides had left soldiers with plummeting morale. There was the devastating Russian defeat at Tannenberg in August 1914 and the German losses in the Battle of the Marne a week later.

By the time winter approached in 1914, and the chill set in, the Western Front stretched hundreds of miles. Countless soldiers were living in misery in the trenches on the fronts, while tens of thousands had already died.

Then Christmas came.

Descriptions of the Christmas Truce appear in numerous diaries and letters of the time. One British soldier, a rifleman named J. Reading, wrote a letter home to his wife describing his holiday experience in 1914: "My company happened to be in the firing line on Christmas Eve, and it was my turn...

to go into a ruined house and remain there until 6:30 on Christmas morning. During the early part of the morning the Germans started singing and shouting, all in good English. They shouted out: 'Are you the Rifle Brigade; have you a spare bottle; if so we will come half way and you come the other half.'"

"Later on in the day they came towards us," Reading described. "And our chaps went out to meet them...I shook hands with some of them, and they gave us cigarettes and cigars. We did not fire that day, and everything was so quiet it seemed like a dream."

Another British soldier, named John Ferguson, recalled it this way: "Here we were laughing and chatting to men whom only a few hours before we were trying to kill!"

Other diaries and letters describe German soldiers using candles to light Christmas trees around their trenches. One German infantryman described how a British soldier set up a makeshift barbershop, charging Germans a few cigarettes each for a haircut. Other accounts describe vivid scenes of men helping enemy soldiers collect their dead, of which there were plenty.

The event proves the power of kindness. War, hatred or ideologies that send men to destroy one another are simply powerless to suppress it. This, to me, is alchemy. It transforms the ugly side of humanity into something beautiful. The world needs it.

Thank You

To my wife, Rita, who has always kept her faith in me and for caring for all our dogs everyday at the old house while I spent most of my time writing.

To my sons, Indiana and Evander, for trying to find the alchemist within themselves.

To my parents, my first teachers of kindness.

To all the people – you know who you are - who have treated me kindly in one way or another

To the Universe...for everything.

About the Author

Leo Alaza is a former newspaper journalist and an Indigenous Peoples activist from Sabah, Island of Borneo. Currently a full-time writer, he has a knack for seeing things differently. One of them is his vision that the new world is a place ruled by kindness. Some people have questioned his belief as being unrealistic to which he often responded by saying, "It's hard for you to believe because you're hearing it from me. Who am I but just one person? But would it become your belief when millions of other people believe it? Over centuries we have blindly accepted many beliefs because societies have made us believe." Leo loves animals who he believes hold the secrets about existence but won't tell us and are amused by our ignorance.

Email: borneotreefish@gmail.com

www.ingramcontent.com/pod-product-compliance
Lightning Source LLC
LaVergne TN
LVHW041114150826
845673LV00007B/2051

* 9 7 9 8 8 9 5 8 8 9 0 3 9 *